Body Language-Master
Alexander The Great

Table of Content

Summary:

This book will take no more than 30 minutes to read. During this time, you will receive maximum information about body language, facial expressions and gestures and learn how to correctly perceive non-verbal information from an interlocutor in any situation.

Phraseological units are a translation from body language

When we want to support our neighbor who is in a difficult situation, we often hug him from the side - so that our shoulder is under his arm, we kind of offer him support.

When curiosity seizes us at the sight of something unfamiliar and unusual, we automatically raise our eyebrows and make big eyes to catch as much information as possible.

Finally, when a person folds his hands in his lap, this does not mean at all that he is shying away from work. It's just that at the moment he really has nothing to do, and his hands lie calmly by themselves.

Body language is our parent language

There is no other human language that is as simple and as honest as body language. With the help of words one can deceive or mislead, but who will be convinced by a forced smile, a fake laugh? The body betrays our true feelings and thoughts, whether we like it or not. People who are well versed in postures, gestures, facial expressions have a great advantage. On the one hand, they effectively use it themselves - after all, a certain signal of the body at the right time can create a miracle. Suffice it to recall timid looks and cautious smiles - an integral part of flirting. On the other hand, they know how to correctly interpret the signals coming from the interlocutor. You will learn exactly how to do this in later chapters.

Body language is far from unambiguous, but "translation" is possible

However, do not think that you are holding a dictionary in your hands that will allow you to "translate", as from a foreign language, any particular gesture or facial expression. An interpretation of body language will always only be a rough "translation". For the best interpretation, three decisive factors must always be kept in mind:• What impression do I make on the interlocutor? Maybe my behavior prompts him to certain conclusions?

• How does my counterpart feel, what is his goal?
• What is the setting in which our meeting takes place?

It is unlikely that you will be able to answer these questions with complete certainty, however, by asking them to yourself, you take a big step towards understanding body signals. This book will help you correctly interpret the movements, postures, gestures and facial expressions of the people with whom you are in contact, both in business and in the private sphere.

I hope you enjoy learning about body language.

1. The relationship and mutual influence of the body and spirit

Just imagine: when we first meet a person, communication is 93 percent through body language. 55 percent of our attention is directed to the posture, gestures and facial expressions of the interlocutor, another 38 percent - to the level of volume and intonation of his voice. The very content of what we hear interests us, compared to the way it is presented, by only 7 percent. And this is not surprising, since the body language of any person says more about his personality than a thousand words.

1.1. Verbal and non-verbal communication

"We can't not communicate." – Making this conclusion, the world-famous psychologist and psychiatrist Paul Watzlawick thought least of all about the verbal possibilities of communication. After all, we constantly report something about ourselves - even when we don't say a word! How do we do it? Through their behavior in certain situations, their manner of communicating with others. It should be emphasized here that, unlike spoken words, body language is almost beyond conscious control.

Nothing gives such direct and truthful information about our sensations, thoughts and experiences as the accompanying gestures and facial expressions.

It's easy to hide behind words if you don't want to tell the truth. Remember how many times you gave assurances that everything is fine with you, and at the same time thought: "It won't get better anyway ..."?

The same language?

There are three kinds of relationship between what you say and how you say it.
• Your behavior confirms your words by sending the same message. No one will doubt your anger if you hit the table with your fist and at the same time express your indignation in suitable speech units. And from a friend who keeps repeating that he is terribly glad to meet you, you have the right to expect a joyful expression on his face.

• Sometimes body language can replace words. Two of the body's most important signals are prime examples here: nodding and shaking the head as an expression of affirmation or denial.

• Finally, in certain situations, your body's signals may contradict your words. In most cases, such a contradiction arises from the fact that you are not saying what you really think and feel.

Slurred messages - two examples

1.Recently, I went to a fashion boutique, where I thoroughly rummaged through things and found myself chic trousers. On the way to the fitting room, a saleswoman caught my eye. The young woman was leaning against the window, her arms folded across her chest. In a monotonous voice, she addressed me with the following speech: "If you need a different size, I'll be happy to help." Having finished with this routine phrase, she began to examine her nails and did not budge when I - without trousers - left the store.

2.A few months before that, I had to be in the role of presenter at the award ceremony for the best innovative business project. The first prize was awarded to a young man who, according to the jury, had invested an exceptionally large amount of time and effort into the development of his idea. At the end of the event, the laureate went up on stage to say a few words. Standing absolutely still, tightly pressing his hands at the seams, he brought to the attention of the public that he was terribly happy with his victory and that it simply did not fit in his head.

Do you see any contradiction in the given examples? Well, of course! The lips (mind) and the body speak different languages here. If someone offers help, it should indicate a willingness to take action. But the figure with arms crossed on his chest produces a completely opposite impression. And it's the same with rapture. From a person who talks about his overwhelming feelings, we also expect appropriate behavior. Because emotional agitation usually finds an outlet in physical mobility - unless we are talking about an extremely timid and reserved person.

Tune in to harmony

What do these simple stories testify to? If a person's words express something very different from their body language, we begin to distrust them. We - albeit unconsciously - perceive such a person as insincere and therefore unsympathetic. So be careful: never try, either by word or outward behavior, to depict something that you do not really think and do not feel. The interlocutor will definitely notice the inconsistency, and he will not have the best opinion about you.

Perhaps your behavior will not betray in the most treacherous way what you are trying to veil with words. However, in any case, it will allow you to draw a conclusion about your sincerity or insincerity. And if you behave illogically, then the interlocutor is unlikely to like you.

1.2. Every body speaks its own language

Everyone is different, so everyone's body language is different. Although we use almost the same gestural and facial signals, the differences between them in the course of non-verbal communication can be quite significant. The main reason is that not everyone is equally inclined to use the body as a mouthpiece for their ideas and impressions.

Two extremes: extrovert and introvert

Observe a pronounced extrovert - his body is charged with energy, mobile, agile. This is manifested both in wide, expressive gestures, directed mainly from oneself, outward, and in extremely expressive facial expressions. Along with a straight posture, this type is characterized by a fast dancing gait.

Introvert looks very different, his external behavior is muffled: little facial expressions, barely noticeable gestures - usually towards himself - and a stooped back. Body language is kept to a minimum and almost nothing is expressed. People of this type can be hard to figure out (but only at first sight).

Body language must match the psychological type

Of course, there are no 100% extroverts and introverts, we are all somewhere between extremes. But no matter what type a person is, his body language should be natural to him. Of course, being naturally timid and indecisive, you can try to act more confident. However, increased gesticulation is unlikely to turn you into a real TV presenter - rather, it will look forced and unnatural.

Because you learn someone else's body language, your personality will not change at all. As a result, you will most likely appear to others as an unattractive pretender.

1.3. The body as a mirror of the soul

Speech and behavior are two different channels through which you communicate with the outside world. And they are by no means isolated from each other. Moreover, thoughts and body language form an inseparable unity and constantly influence each other. By behavior, you can recognize not only your momentary state of mind, but also the experience that you have acquired throughout your life. One way or another, it affects the posture, is expressed in gestures and facial expressions.

Under the weight of a heavy burden...

Imagine a grieving person who has suffered a cruel blow of fate. What image does your imagination paint? It is unlikely that this is a self-confident type, cheerfully walking through life with his head held high. A human being carrying a heavy emotional burden looks literally crushed. The shoulders are lowered, the gaze is directed to the ground, not a drop of energy is felt. The same applies to a person who is depressed. The oppression of negative thoughts slows down all movements, turns the face into a stone mask.

... or in exultation without borders

Positive experiences have the opposite effect. Think about the last time you experienced pure joy. How did you feel, for example, in a state of love or when you managed to conclude an incredibly good deal? I bet you were full of energy and extremely self-confident. And what effect did this mood have on your body language? Surely the shoulders were widely spread, and the gestures were more lively and expressive than usual. And there is no doubt that your radiant face radiated exceptional benevolence.

Everything that a person thinks and feels, everything that he is experiencing at the moment and experienced in a similar situation in the past, inevitably leaves its mark on behavior. A good mood is manifested in a general smartness, a gloomy one bends to the ground.

1.4. Mood as a mirror of the body

As well-being affects behavior, and vice versa: through body language, you can influence your mood. Don't believe? Then try the following exercises:

The body can influence mood

• Imagine that you are very, very sad. Here you sit, dejected and exhausted, hunched over and hanging your head, with the corners of your mouth pulled down. Automatically, you will immediately feel an imaginary weight pressing on your neck. Staying in this position, try to cling to some positive thought - it will not work for anything.

• And now vice versa: straighten up, head up, chest forward, look straight ahead, a smile on your lips. Take a deep breath and try to think of something extremely unpleasant. I highly doubt you can do it easily.

Psychological experiment

The Mannheim psychologist Fritz Strack has been researching the relationship between body language and mood.

He showed funny cartoons to two experimental groups. At the same time, everyone kept a pencil in their mouth: participants in one group had to squeeze it with their lips, and the other with their teeth. And what do you think? What was the reaction of people to funny stories? Those who held the pencil with their teeth laughed heartily, the rest did not laugh at all. You will ask why? And try to do it yourself.

• Hold the pencil between your teeth (lips should not touch it). What's happening? That's it - the corners of your mouth are lifted up, as if you are smiling. Your mood improves by itself.

• Now try to hold the pencil with your lips. You are clearly not laughing. In this position, the mimic muscles of laughter are tightly blocked and do not send signals of joy to the brain.

The following exercises show that body language can not only evoke a particular mood, but also block emotions.

How to use the body to block emotions

• Raise your eyebrows as high as possible, so that your eyes widen a lot, and try to feel the emotion of anger with all its outward manifestations. I guarantee this risky experiment will fail, but you'll have a lot of fun.

• Undoubtedly you will suffer a fiasco even if, moving your eyes from side to side and licking your lips with your tongue, you want to think about something especially unpleasant.

• If you move your eyebrows, then it will be very easy for you to portray indignation. But whether you can smile at the same time or imagine something joyful is a big question.

• Now clench your teeth with all your might and think about a happy future - it's extremely difficult, isn't it?

Body and soul strive for harmony

As you can see, it costs nothing to circle your psyche around your finger. At first, however, there is a feeling of some unnaturalness and pretense, but soon the mood really comes into line with the settings of the body. What is the matter here? What mechanisms make it possible to manipulate the internal state through external posture, facial expressions and gestures? It's very simple: the body associates specific feelings with specific signals. The contraction of certain muscles activates the hormonal system, which adjusts the mood to the signals of the body. After all, the body and soul are constantly aimed at achieving harmony.

Put your knowledge to good use

So, you are convinced that by external behavior you can influence your internal state. Why not take advantage of this knowledge? For example, to improve mental well-being. Or to get rid of a bad mood.

There are several simple tricks to help drive away the blues and tune in to positive thoughts.

Program yourself for the positive

• Simulate the external manifestations of the emotional state you want to achieve.

• Need to de-stress? Then act like you're crazy tired. Lower your shoulders, relax all your muscles, and repeat to yourself that you are completely exhausted.

• Tired of moping? So, first of all, you need to shake yourself physically. Pull yourself up, raise your chin higher and breathe emphasized intensively and rhythmically. You will soon feel much more energized.

• Memories of wonderful and joyful events can work wonders. Try to remember what you felt at that moment, how you behaved, in what position you were. Experience it again, in the same position and with the same feeling of happiness.

Good mood is contagious

If you make a habit of putting yourself in a good mood, it will positively affect those around you. Cheerfulness of spirit and optimism inspire people, including at such events as a presentation or a report.

Body language is the main form of communication.

• At the first meeting, more than 90 percent of the information, on the basis of which a conclusion is made about the possibility of mutual understanding and harmony between the interlocutors, comes through body signals.

• You will only be persuasive if your body language and your speech are in agreement with each other.

• Mood, feelings, experiences always leave an imprint - positive or negative - on your external behavior.

• And vice versa, with the help of certain gestures or facial expressions, you can influence your mental well-being: a calm and free posture, a friendly smile contribute to the emergence of positive thoughts, while negative body signals cause a depressed mood.

1.5. Show your best side!

A familiar situation: you were invited to a celebratory event, and now you enter a room full of strangers. After a few seconds, someone seems pretty to you, but you just don't notice someone. This is natural, because even in the thickest human whirlpool, our evaluative mechanism continues to work hard. We instantly activate 100 billion nerve cells. Even a single signal - for example, a caustic chuckle, a quickly averted look, or a provocative pose of a real macho - makes us immediately form our opinion about a person. The first impression, which has already become a byword, occurs between the mythical 150th millisecond and the 90th second. And it remains decisive. It is interesting that a person listed in the category of "pretty" we automatically ascribe authority in matters that are important to us. And the one who did not like at first sight usually seems to us a person of little knowledge, insignificant, and in the future he will have to prove his competence more than once before our opinion about him changes.

Second impressions are important too!

In a brief moment of the first impression, we are limited to the assessment: "Do you like me or not?" And if someone manages to arouse our sympathy, then the next process starts. As the results of an experiment conducted at the Max Planck Institute for the Psychology of Behavior show, over the next four minutes we carefully follow the person we like, not neglecting - albeit unconsciously - any of the 102 (!) Observation parameters.

Example

What do you think, what do we pay attention to in these four minutes (please note - unconsciously) in the first place? Imagine, for example, a meeting at an interest club, a consumer society meeting, or a queue at a supermarket, bakery, or anywhere else. One of those present - a man or a woman - comes up to you, asks a couple of minor questions, and you strike up a conversation with him / her. And then this is what happens:

• In the first minute, you evaluate the age of the interlocutor, as well as the advantages and disadvantages of his figure, and determine how attractive he is to you.

• On the second and third minutes you are immersed in the details: examine the arms and legs, note the posture and posture, listen to the timbre of the voice and its intonations.

• Not later than the fourth minute expires, you already know for sure whether the interlocutor is nice to you or not. Everything was decided by feelings, without any regard for whether there is already a close man / beloved woman in your life.

How to get the maximum number of "assessment points"

In behavior, a lot is dictated by our nature, and that's good! Stretched body language looks unnatural and does not convince the interlocutor at all. Still, you can try with the help of some "behavioral tricks" to improve the impression we make on others. To do this, you just need to always keep in mind a couple of "golden rules" that help win people's sympathy.

Smile more!

Nothing else can beautify a person like a sincere smile! So remember: not only your lips should smile, but also your eyes. To achieve this, you need to drive away all negative thoughts and replace them with positive ones. Or remember some funny incident.

Your efforts will be rewarded - according to a survey, 68 percent of Germans judge the attractiveness or unattractiveness of new acquaintances by their smile.

In other words: people who often smile and laugh heartily seem more likeable to us, because they radiate cheerfulness and self-confidence.

People with a sense of humor are better at life. They make a career effortlessly and often achieve greater success than hardened grumblers. What is the reason? Scientists have come to the conclusion that even a deliberately stretched smile or just raised eyebrows lead to positive neurophysiological and hormonal reactions.

A happy smile or uncontrollable laughter improves the blood

supply to the brain, maintains a cheerful tone.

A sad or angry facial expression, on the contrary, reduces the oxygen content in the blood. As a result, a vicious circle of mental depression and depression quickly sets in. Therefore, laughter is indeed the best medicine, which, among other things, has the most beneficial effect on our health.

Laughing is good for health

Psychologists who study laughter have found that one minute of contagious laughter has the same strengthening effect as 45 minutes of relaxing auto-training. And only 20 seconds of laughter correspond in their physiological effect to three minutes of rowing.

If you want others to see you as a likeable and competent person, always remember the basic rules regarding body language.

• Show decent posture! You look confident when you stand firmly on the ground. Keep your legs straight, do not bend your knees - you can rely on!

• Control the position of the head! Keep your head straight all the time. It gives the impression of calm dignity and objectivity. But be careful with your chin! A bulging chin will immediately give you an arrogant and unsympathetic look.

• Don't forget your hands! Arms crossed on the chest - the position is certainly comfortable, but it signals detachment and isolation. Agree that openness and willingness to communicate cause disposition much more.

• Keep your distance! Each person lives in his own "spatial cocoon", providing him with a certain comfort zone. It is different for everyone, but usually approximately equal to the length of an outstretched arm. For close people, however, we make an exception and do not strain at all when they violate this distance. Therefore, if you communicate with a person whom you do not yet know very well, you must respect the boundaries of his

individual space. Otherwise, there is a danger of appearing intrusive.

2. Posture is your business card

Have you ever watched some young people "walk through life"? Shuffling gait, with a stooped back, a protruding belly and a lowered head? What do you think is the issue here?

2.1. What you need to know about posture

Best of all, a person's personality is reflected in his posture. Gesticulation and facial expressions, of course, are also marked by individual features, but for the most part they are determined by the situation. And in the manner of standing, walking or sitting, it is quite possible to draw some conclusions about our inner world.

Youth tends to seek support

How to decipher the posture that we see in many young people? Try to remember your attitude at the age when you were in the process of becoming and the question of which path to choose in life remained unresolved and painful. In other words: the personality has not yet matured, has not taken shape. The same can be said about posture - she clearly lacks self-confidence. As soon as this indicative phase passes, the posture will also change - it will become the hallmark of the personality. From the introductory chapter, you already know what the manner of keeping your back straight or, conversely, slouching means. This means that they are quite capable of reading messages sent through body language by standing, sitting or walking people.

2.2. What does it mean to stand correctly and how to learn it

It is enough to carefully look at the person standing in front of us - and we can safely assume what type of personality he belongs to.

What does standing posture mean?

• If someone cannot stand still, shifts from foot to foot all the time, this means that he does not have a definite point of view. Such a person, most likely, is not self-confident, does not seek to defend his opinion, or often changes it.

• On the other hand, if a person stands rooted to the spot and barely moves, then it is fair to conclude that he is too rigid, too inflexible - both in behavior and in outlook on life.

• You already know what message your stooped posture sends about a person. A hunched back and a lowered head have long been a symbol of despondency, depression and impotence.

• A completely different impression is formed when we see freely straightened shoulders, a slightly raised head and a direct look. Then the whole outward appearance of a person testifies to a high self-consciousness and self-esteem and suggests the great inner freedom inherent in him.

About one small difference

Have you ever noticed that women tend to put their weight on their left foot when they are standing, while men often use their right foot as the supporting foot? This phenomenon can be explained. The fact is that the activity of each of the two hemispheres of our brain is connected with the opposite side of the body. Moreover, the right hemisphere is responsible for such "typically feminine" qualities as creativity or emotionality, and the left hemisphere is responsible for the "purely masculine" ability for logic and analytical thinking. For this reason, women concentrate mainly on the left side of the body, men on the right.

Nowadays, this rule is no longer so unambiguous. But having established which leg of the person of interest to us - regardless of his gender - is the supporting one, we can well conclude that he belongs mainly to the emotional or rational type.

Reception "Crown and pea" to develop the correct posture

In the first chapter, you read about the importance of good posture. And, of course, you want to know how to learn to stand in order to make a favorable impression? The answer is simple: with the help of a technique called "Crown and Pea".

• Place your feet so that the distance between them is approximately the width of your hips. Legs put one to another give the impression of insecurity, spaced too wide - they speak of frivolity.

• Pull your shoulders back slightly. Lowered and protruding shoulders are a sign of despondency and impotence.

• Body weight should be evenly distributed on both legs. If you constantly shift from foot to foot, your interlocutor or listener will be nervous and doubt your competence.

• Finally, imagine that you have a pea in your pope and a crown on your head.

These imaginary aids will help you, firstly, to give your muscles the necessary tension and, secondly, to avoid dangerous lifting of the chin up. After all, with a high chin, you will not only appear to others as an arrogant and unpleasant type, but you will also lose your crown.

When the audience looks at us

Are you going to give a public speech or a presentation? Of course, you have no desire to show your excitement to those present. From "stage fever" simple physical exercises usually help

- they put thoughts in order and relieve stiffness in posture.

• Are you experiencing a lot of inner tension? Then tense your body too - literally every muscle! After a few seconds, relax while exhaling forcefully. If you repeat this exercise two or three times, not only physical tightness will disappear, but also mental anxiety.

• Probably, you no longer remember how, in your distant childhood, your mother rocked you before going to bed. It's a pity, because otherwise you would not have lost the knowledge of how soothing the lulling movement. Still try to take advantage of it. Stand firmly on both feet and slowly rock back and forth. Gradually, the pulse and breathing will slow down and the excitement will pass.

Where to put your hands?

So, you know what should be the posture during a speech in front of an audience. But what to do with the hands? There are two solutions to the problem.

1. Freely lower your arms along the body - this looks the most natural.

2. Bend your arms freely, holding them at about waist height. At the same time, you must be ready at the right time to back up your words with explanatory gestures.

What to avoid

• Do not put your hands behind your back - this posture expresses secrecy and passivity.

• Keep your hands out of your pockets. Hidden hands mean a threat or self-doubt.

• Do not fold your lowered hands in front of you, turned palms inward. This "footballer's posture before a free kick" also speaks of hesitation and doubt.

• Do not rest your hands on your hips - in this position, a person, as it were, claims for additional space, and at the same time for a dominant role.

With an imaginary crown on your head and a pea in your butt, your posture will be the most optimal. In this case, it is best to lower your hands freely. From excessive excitement and tightness, exercises to change tension and relaxation help.

By the way

How confident and dignified a pose will look - regardless of whether you are standing or sitting - is largely determined by the costume. So always choose clothing that you feel comfortable in, that suits your personality and suits the situation. Without being distracted by equipment and without constantly fiddling with a dress, you can fully concentrate on communication and will not cause the impression of stiffness in your interlocutors.

2.3. Are you sure you can sit?

Not only posture, but also the manner of sitting can tell a lot about us. During a conversation (business or personal - it does not matter), the posture of the person sitting opposite helps to better understand his mood and his point of view. A few examples.

What can be guessed from the posture of a seated person

• Does your interlocutor lean forward slightly? Thus, it signals interest in you and your words.

• Does the interlocutor turn to you slightly sideways, exposing his shoulder? He is probably not (yet) interested in you or (yet) not imbued with trust in you.

• If the interlocutor leans back in his chair, he, most likely, either critically evaluates your opinion, or does not accept it at all. However, this may also mean that your arguments convinced him and he says goodbye to his own ideas.

• The interlocutor turns away - this is a formal refusal to accept your offer.

• A person tilting his head slightly to his shoulder exposes his weak spot - the carotid artery. Such a tilt of the head, accompanied by a smile, sends an unambiguous signal: "You can trust me!"

• When you see that the interlocutor is sitting on the very edge of the chair, you can be almost one hundred percent sure that he is about to leave. This person is in a hurry and therefore not overly receptive to what you are saying.

• On the contrary, the one who firmly occupies the entire surface of the seat - and his shins form a strictly vertical line - or draws his legs under the seat of the chair, demonstrates complete readiness for specific actions.

• Legs stretched forward indicate that the person feels comfortable and is far from the idea of quickly getting up and leaving - with this position, this is hardly possible at all.

• Looking at a person who has crossed his legs, pay attention to what direction the leg placed on top takes. If she is facing the interlocutor, this can be interpreted as a sign of consent.

• Tightly clenched knees indicate that the person is experiencing doubts and insecurity.

What to do with hands?

During a conversation, we, as a rule, do not perform any actions, which means that we do not seem to need hands. Therefore, we either put them on the armrests, or fold them freely on our knees. Another option is to cross them on the chest. This posture is often misinterpreted as defensive. However, this is not quite true. Sometimes arms crossed on the chest can indeed serve as a signal of rejection of the situation. But still, first of all, this means that at the moment a person is not going to do anything and is only waiting for how further events will unfold. Despite the completely harmless meaning, this position is not suitable for business negotiations. Why - you can learn from an impressive experiment conducted in the United States.

Arms folded across the chest reduce the ability to perceive

In one of the lectures, American students were asked to sit with their arms folded across their chests and legs crossed outstretched. As a result, these students learned 38 percent less information than their classmates who listened to the same lecture in a free position. That is, this position of the body not only gives the impression of complete isolation and readiness for defense, but also significantly impairs the ability to acquire new knowledge.

Movement activates mental activity

Often, after a rather lengthy discussion of some issues at a round table - this is especially true for business negotiations - the discussion comes to a standstill, as individual participants in the discussion, without accepting any arguments, continue to insist on their point of view. It has nothing to do with stubbornness. The reason is this: if the body remains in the same position for a long time, this is bad for the flexibility of thinking. The way out is to create conditions for changing postures. We need to give people the opportunity to move around, for example, arrange a short break. Often fixed thoughts disappear along with the fixed posture.

The sitting posture should be as open as possible, arms should not be crossed over the chest or legs crossed. An open posture not only improves your receptivity to new information, but also has a positive effect on your image. Others perceive you as a sociable, cheerful and active person.

2.4. That's how it "goes"

In order to make a favorable impression on others, along with the correct posture, it is necessary to take care of a free, natural gait. When walking, also keep straight - this indicates openness and self-confidence. In a person who walks with his head hanging and barely taking his feet off the ground, it is difficult to imagine energy and a firm character. However, avoid the extreme - to walk "as if swallowed an arshin." In this case, people look constrained and inflexible.

What does it mean to "keep yourself right"

Take note of a couple of important rules. By adhering to them, you will be sure that you behave in society, especially in a business environment, with due dignity.

• When you're walking toward a target—whether it's a podium, a stage microphone, another person, or a group of people—move purposefully but at a normal pace (don't run, but don't slow either). The width of the step should correspond to your height (do not mince, but do not turn the steps into seven-league ones). At the same time, make sure that your breathing remains even.

• When entering a room, do not stop with a timid look on the threshold, otherwise you will look like you want to quickly turn around and leave. Take a few steps into the interior of the room, quickly orient yourself and determine the goal of your further advancement: an unoccupied chair, a good friend, or something else.

Keeping distance is a guarantee of safety

Imagine that a certain subject approaches you and stops right in front of your nose, almost close to you. How will you react? Your muscles will automatically tighten and you will step back slightly. Why? Because you feel discomfort and some kind of threat. Each person defines several "safety zones" for himself, depending on who he communicates with. When the boundaries of personal space are violated, our body instinctively assumes a defensive posture. In general, there are three psychologically justified communication distances.

Three distances of communication

1. **Intimate:**This is the space around us, described by the radius of an outstretched arm. Only close people have access to this zone: parents, children, spouses, etc. If an outsider invades it, for example, in an overcrowded bus or a crowded elevator, we try to maintain a distance conditionally, avoiding direct eye contact, looking at the floor or somewhere far away.

2. **Personal:**It involves increasing the distance between interlocutors up to 120 cm. This is a zone of communication with family members, friends and acquaintances.

3. **Social:** Here, approximately 3 meters are added to the intimate distance. We set such a communication distance for ourselves when we perform one of our social roles - for example, the role of a responsible employee, manager, seller or buyer.

By the way

If someone comes close from the front, head-on, you experience the violation of your personal space more acutely than when you are approached from the side - the person feels less vulnerable from the side.

The straight back of a walking person expresses dignity and self-confidence. Measure the width of your step with your height, approach people or objects with a firm gait. Be sure to respect the boundaries of the personal space of others. No one likes it when someone shamelessly "presses" on him.

2.5. Signs of flirting

There are situations when the ability to understand the body language of those with whom we communicate becomes especially desirable and valuable. Especially when we are dealing with people whom we hardly or do not know at all. For example, when establishing new business contacts or new personal acquaintances. This skill is extremely important if we are trying to make a good impression on the person who has interested us. How do you feel when you first meet? You are probably nervous, worried, shy. This is because you don't know what thoughts are going through the mind of a new acquaintance. How do I appear to him? What if I'm doing something wrong? But you can find the answer to a number of such questions if you carefully observe the behavior of your counterpart. Certain body signals will let you know that the interlocutor, although (still) unconsciously,

Positive signals at the first meeting

• If someone tries to be close to you all the time, this is a good sign. Sitting opposite, he may, for example, lean slightly towards you, or his thrown leg may be directed in your direction.

• Men, when they want to please, like to demonstrate a jolly bearing, stick out their chest and draw in their stomach. In a sitting position, legs wide apart speak of the same thing - a pose that claims significant additional space.

• When women want to show their best side, they keep their back and shoulders straight and throw their hair back to show their neck and face in a favorable light. At the same time, they look, on the one hand, spectacular, on the other - defenseless (the cervical artery is the most vulnerable spot). Thus, they remind of the weakness of the fair sex and awaken the instinct of a protector in men.

• Sitting down on a chair or in an armchair, women also tend to behave as gracefully as possible. The sight of a seated woman is especially charming if her knees are closed, and her legs are set a little obliquely.

The more often a person turns to you, the more he is interested in a close acquaintance. If he takes one of the positions described above, your prospects are more than tempting.

Posture is your calling card.

• *Whether you are walking, standing, or sitting, always stay straight.*

• *How to stand correctly will teach you the "Crown and Pea" technique. At the same time, the top of the head stretches upward, the chest rises slightly and the muscles of the abdomen and buttocks tighten.*

• *When you are standing, your arms should be freely lowered along the body. Remember that they should be kept in sight at all times.*

• *It is recommended to sit in an open position, facing the person you are talking to. The tilt of the body or the direction of the thrown leg towards the interlocutor is evidence of sympathy.*

• *When walking, pay attention to the pace (it should not be too fast, but not too slow) and the firmness of the step.*

• *In the process of communication, note the signs of sympathy sent by the interlocutor, for example, a head bowed to the shoulder.*

• Maintain the necessary muscle tension, but at the same time remain mobile, otherwise you will look like a mannequin.

3. Gestures - what your hands say

Have you ever had to communicate with a person whose hands would remain absolutely motionless during a conversation? I don't think so. After all, gesticulation is one of the integral components of communication, moreover, it is difficult to consciously regulate it.

3.1. The basics of gestures

Gesticulation itself is a kind of language. There are over 5000 different gestures in the world. They serve primarily to reinforce and complement what we say. But sometimes certain hand movements reveal the true meaning of the words and may even indicate a lie. In such cases, we speak of "treacherous gestures."

Naturally, each person gesticulates in his own way, depending on age, gender, nationality or personal temperament. However, there are a few general rules, the knowledge of which will help you better understand the interlocutor.

What secrets are given out by gestures

• Pay attention to which hand the person is using to gesticulate. A certain hemisphere of the brain is responsible for choosing the right or left hand, as we have already seen in the case of the supporting leg. If a person gesticulates with his right hand, we can conclude that logical thinking prevails in him. If left, then we most likely have an emotional nature.

• The direction of gestures is also quite eloquent. In open, sociable and sincere people, hand movements, as a rule, go outward from themselves. In closed and restrained people, we usually see the opposite picture.

• Self-confidence is expressed primarily in energetic and decisive gestures. Nervous and inconsistent gestures betray tension and uncertainty - just imagine a person who is constantly scratching or fiddling with clothes. And the one who almost or does not gesticulate looks completely timid and shy.

• A person rubbing his hands or stroking his shoulder feels the need for friendly participation, but is forced to be content with this surrogate gesture, since there is no one nearby who would be sincerely disposed towards him.

Hands are our most important tool, without which we could not perform the most simple and familiar actions. Not surprisingly, their role in communication is irreplaceable. Gestures can tell a lot both about ourselves (our thoughts and feelings) and about the interlocutor.

• Hands tightly clenched into fists - a sign of extreme indignation, frustration.

• Clenched hands, directed towards the interlocutor, speak of the desire to convince of their readiness to do everything possible.

• House-shaped hands demonstrate confidence in their words and self-confidence.

• If the interlocutor calmly puts his hands behind his back, he wants to show you his superiority.

• Upturned open palms mean that the person is ready to both give and receive. With this gesture, he confirms what was said or unconsciously asks the other for confirmation.

• Grasping one's own wrist usually expresses frustration.

• If the hand slides from the wrist to the shoulder, we can confidently assume that the person falls into a rage and aggression.

• "Pistol" - pointing the index finger at the interlocutor - is also considered a sign of aggression. In addition, this gesture is very authoritarian.

• If the clasped fingers suddenly straighten like a hedgehog, this should be taken as an intention to defend.

What are the fingers talking about?

No less eloquent than the gestures of our hands, and at least as varied can be the movements of individual fingers or their combinations.

*Thumb.*With the help of the thumb, we achieve maximum force and use it when we want to literally squeeze or crush something. Therefore, is it any wonder that in body language it also symbolizes power and strength and, in comparison with other fingers, occupies the most "authoritative" position.

*Forefinger.*Along with the thumb, the index finger also plays an important role in gesticulation, if only because it is used by us most often. Usually it serves to express the will or willingness to act. However, depending on the position of the finger, the meanings of statements can vary greatly.

*Middle finger.*The longest of our fingers is usually associated with a sense of self-respect and pride.

*Ring finger.*The ring finger is closely associated with our feelings, which is not at all surprising. Watch a person who is overwhelmed with emotions.

*Little finger.*In body language, the little finger plays a far from negligible role, since it is able to express a lot. By the little finger, you can determine the attitude of a person to the interlocutor or his feelings in a certain situation.

The individual way of gesticulating allows us to learn a lot about the personality and intentions of the interlocutor. People of the emotional type tend to use their left hand for gestures, while the rational type use their right hand. Open gestures, directed away from yourself and upwards, indicate a sociable, self-confident person.

3.2. Positive and negative meaning of gestures

Often gestures are so expressive that they do not need any additional explanation. Everyone knows what a thumbs up means, and everyone understands what a person wants to say by touching his temple with his index finger.

Many simple gestures are also perceived by us as positive or negative signs - this happens completely unconsciously, but it significantly affects the communication process. If you pay due attention to gestures, you can make a much greater impression on your counterpart, as well as more accurately assess his intentions.

What gestures should be avoided

Try not to use gestures that evoke negative associations.

• If your hands are out of sight of the interlocutor, it is bad for communication. Hands thrust into pockets indicate indifference, and hidden behind the back or under the table - about the desire to hide something important. All this contributes little to the emergence of mutual trust.

• Gesticulation below the waistline always has a tinge of vulgarity and bad manners.

• Gestures directed from top to bottom express rejection, rejection and denial - that is, the person is rather pessimistic. In addition, such a hand movement is often perceived as bossy, imperative.

• Never point at someone or something with your index finger or pencil - it gives a negative impression. Both the finger and the pencil seem to claim a dominant role and carry a certain threat, almost like a real weapon. It is unlikely that anyone will like it.

• Arms crossed on the chest, turned back forward - a sign of isolation.
• Apologetic gestures, such as shrugging the shoulders and turning the hands palms up at the same time, create a sense of helplessness and lack of autonomy.

What gestures should be adopted

If you manage to do without negative gestures, then the impression you make on others will be at least neutral. However, with some unambiguously positive gestures, it's not hard to get yourself seen as a likeable and trustworthy person.

• Hands should always be in sight - then the interlocutor will feel more confident.

• Gesticulation above the waist line is a sign of good parenting.

• Gestures directed from the bottom up indicate great interest, even admiration, and arouse a reciprocal interest in the interlocutor.

• Open gestures, such as palms up, usually show sincerity and directness of intention, signaling a willingness to give, but at the same time to receive. This is especially important if you are making a commercial offer to a partner.

Gestures should match both your character and the situation.

When accompanying speech with positive gestures, be sure to keep in mind: gestures should be in harmony with your personality and be appropriate in this particular situation. If a businesslike, somewhat reserved person suddenly starts waving his arms violently, then it will certainly look rather comical. On the contrary, timid, indecisive movements are not at all suitable for people of an extraverted type. Equally important is the environment. Sweeping, overly emotional gestures in a conversation with one or two interlocutors are perceived as excessive exaggeration. But when you're speaking in front of a large group of people, the gestures need to be as clear as possible so that everyone can see and understand them.

If you want to significantly improve the impression you make on others, you must deeply feel the difference between positive and negative gestures. The main rule boils down to the following: open, upward gestures above the waist line contribute to the formation of a positive opinion. At the same time, gestures should correspond to your personality type and specific situation.

3.3. Are you saying hello right?

A lot depends on the first impression! You have already met with this statement more than once and probably managed to notice that it is by no means taken from the ceiling. It only takes a few seconds to form a judgment about a person we see for the first time. And here everything matters. Among other things, the role of the first handshake should not be underestimated. In business communication, already in the manner of a partner to greet those present, you can learn a lot about him: about his intentions, his self-esteem and his position. Some psychologists even believe that the success or failure of the upcoming transaction depends on the correct handshake.

What can you tell about a person by their handshake?

• A firm handshake corresponds to a strong character - a person is clearly confident in his abilities.

• In contrast, a sluggish handshake, in which the fingers do not fully extend and the other person's hand is not fully grasped, is characteristic of people who are insecure.

• A person who decisively holds out his hand so that the palms are deeply inserted into each other, as if he wants to say: "I am ready to discuss any issues."

• If someone, when shaking hands, leaves a gap between the palms, this means that although he is, in principle, an open person, for the time being he does not intend to reveal all his cards.

• In the same way, the one who gives you an unbending palm or just his fingers for a handshake prefers (for now) to keep a certain distance.

• A few outstretched fingers instead of a hand indicate that the person is rather indifferent to the upcoming negotiations.

• If your hand is pulled down with force when shaking hands, you are dealing with an imperious nature.

• The habit of leadership is also manifested in someone who, at the same time as shaking hands with his free hand, touches your forearm - this gesture signals the desire to lead you.

• But when the free hand of the person you are greeting rests on top of your shaking hand, this expresses his special respect.

• Shaking an outstretched hand with both hands - the so-called "gesture of small shopkeepers" - gives the appearance of close acquaintance and complete trust of the relationship, but in fact it does not look very nice.

Attention: never forget about the distance of communication!

You must respect the boundaries of the personal space of the person you are greeting. This means that the distance between you should be at least the length of an outstretched arm.

For a neutral greeting, simply raise your hand vertically - without much affectation, but not sluggishly. The handshake should be neither too firm nor too loose.

3.4. Traitor Gestures

Remember your childhood. As a child, you probably liked to add something to your stories sometimes. But you have always been exposed by a characteristic gesture - which one? Correctly! You raised your hand to your lips, as if belatedly trying to stop the lies coming out of your mouth.

Growing up, we naturally try to unlearn this too eloquent habit, but the subconscious reflex remains with us all our lives.

This reflex is clearly manifested in situations where we do not say what we think, or we are trying to seriously deceive someone. We no longer hold our hand in front of our lips - we are betrayed by completely different traitorous gestures.

Observe the interlocutor: does he really think exactly what he says?
And turn on self-control: perhaps, imperceptibly for yourself, you

have learned some of the traitor gestures listed below.

Gestures that should alert us

• In principle, any touching of a person's face or neck, after he has spoken, indicates that he did not say everything or told a lie. The reflex movement here simply takes on a different direction, and the speaker, instead of bringing his hand to his lips, for example, rubs the bridge of his nose.

• Restless movements, when someone constantly adjusts his clothes, touches jewelry or other objects with his fingers, means an absolute unwillingness to vouch for the truthfulness of his words.
• Someone who verbally agrees with you (accepts your offer) but simultaneously makes a gesture of rejection (for example, brushes a speck of dust off his clothes, puts a pencil or other object aside, or rubs his hand over his lips) shows that he In fact, he is far from in solidarity with you.

• "I'm open to any suggestions!" - If a person pronounces this phrase and at the same time folds his hands with a lock, then one should hardly take his words seriously.

• An interlocutor who, listening to you, touches his earlobe, most likely does not completely agree with what you are saying. Such a gesture is called "punishing".

• If the speaker constantly pulls his hair or holds his hand to his mouth, he seems to us timid and indecisive.

• A person promises us to fix something, to take care of something, to assist in something, and at the same time crosses his arms over his chest or puts them in his pockets - you can be sure that in reality he is not going to do anything.

Attention! Touching the face or neck after the expressed opinion, you cause in the interlocutor a subconscious distrust of yourself.

3.5. A little more about the signs of flirting

In one of the previous chapters, you already got acquainted with the signals that help you start a business relationship or communicate with a person you like. Attention! Some of the gestures that we have just classified as "treacherous" have a completely different meaning in a flirting situation.

Gestures expressing sympathy

• Men often touch their face when they find a woman attractive.

• The way a man handles a woman's hand can tell a lot about his true feelings. If he touches exclusively her fingertips, then most likely he prefers (yet) not to go closer. If he completely covers her hand with his own, then he expresses his ardent sympathy and desire for a more intimate relationship.

• Women often touch the shoulder of the interlocutor they like.

• Brushing away non-existent specks or smoothing out his clothes, a person "in the context of flirting" demonstrates only his desire to look well-groomed and neat.

In addition, the gestures of flirting men and women allow us to guess some of their personality traits.

Gestures will say: macho or mumbling ...

• A man who keeps his hands in his pants pockets would like to look "cool", but in fact he lacks determination.

• If a man squeezes his elbow from time to time, be on the lookout. It is difficult for him to cope with life circumstances, he feels helpless. He dreams of finding a woman who would always support him.

• Hands folded behind the back is a good sign. It can be assumed that this man knows his worth and keeps the situation under control.

• If he puts his index finger on his cheek, and the middle one on his chin, then this means that the woman has completely captured his attention. You can also add that such a man, at least occasionally, is able to admit his mistakes.

…or the woman of your dreams

• A woman who never stops gesturing nervously for a minute is likely to have an indecisive nature and very little interest in a serious relationship.

• On the contrary, a woman who constantly straightens her hair or, for example, wraps a strand around her finger, shows genuine interest in a man. This gesture also allows us to conclude that she is sensitive and capable of empathy.

From the movements of the hands, one can draw some conclusions about the personality of a person, as well as about his mood at the moment.

• *Gestures directed upward from oneself speak of optimism and sincerity.*

• *Closed people gesticulate little and usually towards themselves.*

• *Gestures below the waist line give a frivolous impression.*

• *A firm handshake indicates self-confidence, a sluggish handshake indicates the opposite.*

• If a person verbally agrees, but at the same time fiddling with his clothes, fiddling with objects in his hands, or touching his face and neck, you should be wary: he is not saying what he thinks.

• However, in a situation of flirting, the opposite is true: somewhat feigned concern for one's appearance and touching one's face mean interest and sympathy.

4. Mimicry is a mirror of the soul

The patterns of human facial expressions are a whole science. Neither posture, nor posture, nor gestures give such a complete and definite idea of our feelings and experiences as facial expressions. This is closely related to the large number of facial muscles (there are 43 in total) - in no other place in the human body will we find such an accumulation of muscles in a relatively small area. Thanks to this unique equipment of the face, a huge variety of facial expressions is provided. Many differ from each other only in small nuances.

4.1. Alpha and omega of our facial expressions

There are 250,000 facial expressions recorded in the world. According to them, people of different nationalities determine the state of mind of their loved ones. However, the number of facial messages that do not depend on individual character, gender, nationality and cultural affiliation is not at all so large. All of them correlate with the basic emotions of a person and are quite easy to decipher.

This is what a rejection looks like - respond to it correctly

Imagine that you have just made an offer to a person or put forward your conditions and now you are waiting for his consent. If he closes his lips tightly and keeps his head straight and still, then you have nothing to hope for. This facial expression signals a complete lack of understanding, and in the worst case, even resentment. A tightly closed mouth is a sign that the interlocutor has ceased to perceive your words.

Similarly, a person who, listening to you, wrinkles his nose and closes his eyes, thereby clearly demonstrates his disagreement: by reducing the visibility zone, we unconsciously distance ourselves from what we hear.

What to do in this situation? Show that you are trustworthy by tilting your head slightly to the side and smiling. This should convince the interlocutor of the absence of aggression on your part and defuse the situation.

... so - consent

If the interlocutor raises his eyebrows in response to your statement, you can assume that he is interested. Why? We automatically seek out additional information about what we found interesting. At the same time, we raise our eyebrows high so that our eyes become larger and can perceive more visual information.

... and so - utmost attention

Have you ever watched the expression on the face of a child sitting in front of the TV and completely absorbed in any program? Yes, yes, you are right! Focused gaze and open mouth. Such facial expressions often appear on the faces of adults and mean that at the moment we do not want and cannot be distracted by some extraneous matters, because all attention is focused on only one thing.

A child, captured by the spectacle, will not respond to questions and even to reproaches of the mother - he is simply not capable of action. This is confirmed by the following small experiment: open your mouth and count how much is 13 × 4. You will have to work hard.

Mimic folds are a sign of tension

Here is another example that proves that certain facial expressions can limit our ability to act.

Have you ever sat at your desk for hours while thinking about a problem, but did not move forward a single step? If in this situation you could look at yourself from the outside, you would see your frowning forehead with sharply marked folds - this is how mental tension is unconsciously reflected on the face.

But it is precisely this facial expression that paradoxically blocks mental activity, sending signals of doubt and hesitation to the brain. As a result, thoughts become even more critical and inflexible, and, finally, you find yourself in a complete dead end. There is only one way out of it - relax your face!

Read my lips!

Most often, we try to read the thoughts of the interlocutor in his eyes. However, the mouth is also able to express a lot, and not only in the process of speaking.

The shape, tension, position of the lips often betray what a person would like to hide.

• The raised corners of a mouth testify to cheerful, easy character.

• The corners of the mouth, lowered down, on the contrary, are always inherent in something preoccupied, pessimistic people.

• A person with full lips is characterized by strong emotions - he experiences joy, sadness, and anger in its entirety.

• Delicately defined small lips indicate a person's ability to sophisticated, refined feelings - right on the proverb "Better less, but better."

• A protruding lower lip most likely belongs to a person prone to impulsive reactions, and often to rash acts. Such people live by the principle: "The main thing is to get involved in the battle, and then we'll see."

• If the upper lip protrudes forward, then this indicates delicacy, sensitivity and a predisposition to intense experiences.

• You see that the interlocutor twisted his mouth. This means that he has not yet fully understood the issue and decided to postpone the final decision for the time being.

• Alternately licking the upper and lower lips suggests that the person is enjoying the way things are going, or that they are enjoying the situation.

• But if he runs his tongue only along the lower lip, then this indicates reflection.

• Calmly relaxed lips correspond to a calmly relaxed state of mind, such a person will act independently and flexibly.

• You can guess from the tightly compressed lips of the interlocutor that he does not perceive your arguments. He holds a different opinion and internally closed himself off from you - this was immediately reflected in his posture and facial expressions.

• If he firmly decided to reject your proposal, you can find out about it by the protruding lower lip.

• Your counterpart made a movement with his tongue forward - mentally he moved something away from himself.

• Smiling with only one side of the mouth can indicate either internal discord or sarcasm.

• The interlocutor's lips are tense - this signal also has two interpretations: the person is frightened and prefers to withdraw himself, or he is irritated and angry.

A small digression. How to keep your head?

In the process of communication, one should pay attention not only to facial expressions, that is, to the facial expression of the interlocutor, but also to the position of his head - it can be quite eloquent.

• If a person holds his head straight and turns his whole body towards you, he demonstrates his readiness to fight. And if, in addition, his gaze glides over your head, take this as a warning: "I can see perfectly what is happening here."

• The head tilted to the shoulder is a completely different matter. This sign is perceived as a desire for harmonious relationships. They send you a signal: "You can trust me."

• However, some additional nuances give this tilt of the head a completely different meaning. Therefore, try to consider all possible options. For example, a look directed from the bottom up, one raised eyebrow and wrinkled forehead is more a sign of distrust.

Feel relaxed

Studies show that cheerful, smiling people are much more resourceful than those who constantly frown.
Relaxation of the facial muscles helps to relieve internal tension, and in addition prevents the appearance of wrinkles.

From time to time it is useful to do light gymnastics for the face. I offer you

3 simple exercises:

1. Raise your eyebrows as high as you can and then relax.

2. Close your eyes tightly and open your eyes again.

3. Wrinkle your nose for a few seconds and make your lips look like a bow.

Repeat the exercises several times. It will be great if you laugh heartily at your grimaces - laughter gives a feeling of happiness!

The number of facial expressions is truly countless. However, the basic human emotions - such as grief, joy or surprise - look the same in any nation and are easily "read". You can recognize the refusal by the tightly compressed lips of the interlocutor, the consent - by his open look. Attention: by relaxing the mimic muscles of the face, you liberate your thoughts.

4.2. Positive and negative meaning of facial expressions

The visual impression of communication with a person remains in memory longer than the verbal one. As for facial expressions, here, as in gestures, negative effects should be avoided.

Mimic, which is better to refuse

• Most people who have just experienced stress have an angry, displeased expression on their face. Smiling in such a situation will help you ease the emotional tension and look more attractive and charming.

• Inflated lips are quite capable of having the expected impact on a loved one: change his intentions, induce him to agree. But in public life, in business contacts, such a facial expression is completely inappropriate.

• The same applies to the protruding tongue - this facial expression is generally below any criticism.

• A crooked smile does not look very attractive either, when only one corner of the mouth is raised. With such a mine on your face, you can easily arouse suspicions not only of insincerity, but also of cynicism.

• And remember the main rule: never try to consciously change your facial expressions, if you do not want to leave the interlocutors with an unpleasant impression of artificiality and pretense.

Please smile!

There is only one tool that can absolutely guarantee that others will appreciate you in the highest degree positively, and that tool is a simple smile. But she must be sincere! It is not enough just to stretch your lips - you need to smile with your whole face. Raised cheeks, small wrinkles around the eyes, calmly lowered eyebrows - these are the sure signs of a real, unfeigned smile.

The advantage of a joyful facial expression is also that it causes positive neurophysiological, and as a result, hormonal reactions in the body.

Thanks to a sincere smile, you really come into a great mood. This is a simple technique that helps to cheer yourself up in just a few seconds.

The nod works!

Body signals that always work positively, especially in a negotiation setting, include an affirmative nod. With an encouraging nod, you encourage the interlocutor to further statements, show him your attention and confirm his words. This gesture can be strengthened by accompanying it with suitable approving interjections.

In our cultural space, a nod signifies agreement. When we answer a question in the affirmative, we not only say yes, but at the same time we make the corresponding movement of the head.

Watch the speeches of politicians or some kind of round table on TV. Expressing his opinion, a person automatically nods.

If among the participants in the conversation there are people who think the same way, then soon these "allies" also begin to nod - as if to agree.

Therefore, when you present your point of view to the interlocutor and want to convince him, accompany the speech with a slight nod. This will increase your chances of getting his approval. And you will know that he shares your position even before he starts talking - yes, yes, precisely by affirmative nods.

In the context of flirting

Someone sends you a friendly smile - well, that's a good sign anyway. However, eye contact plays a decisive role.

If a person stops his gaze at you for an exaggeratedly long time, then this can be perceived as an unambiguous manifestation of interest.

Make sure that in stressful situations, the expression of gloomy hopelessness does not freeze on your face. Free your facial expressions, and with it your thoughts.
Never resort to fake facial expressions, otherwise you will look

unnatural. And most importantly, smile!

4.3. One glance is enough

"My look tells everything"—at least a lot. If we imagine how one person can look at another, or how the expression of the eyes can change in certain situations, then we can easily agree that sometimes this is more eloquent than any words.

When meeting, it is often the first seconds of visual contact that play a decisive role.

Depending on how you look at a person, he will consider you attractive or unpleasant.

What is able to express a look

• For a look to be truly friendly and open, it must be accompanied by a slight smile. Such eye contact, lasting for several moments, indicates interest and at the same time characterizes you as a confident and trustworthy person.

• A quick, attentive look indicates that you noticed a person and appreciated him.

• A look, tensely fixed on the floor, gives the impression of self-absorption and lack of interest in others.

• If you do not "dignify" the interlocutor with a look and look past you all the time, he will consider you a self-confident and arrogant type.

• More than unpleasant "drilling" - a long and stubborn - look. It causes us anxiety and a desire to go somewhere far away.

• For those who wear glasses: avoid looking at the interlocutor over glasses, otherwise you will look like a strict teacher, and this does not contribute to effective communication, especially in business negotiations.

• Focused squinted look indicates an aggressive attitude and a desire to attack. Hardly anyone will like it.

"Evil eye"

An unblinking gaze has an effect on our inner state.

Watch, on occasion, how the muscles of the neck tense up, how the breathing slows down and becomes more shallow when you direct an unkind, concentrated look at someone. With such facial expressions, signals about a potential threat enter your brain, and you kind of put yourself on "full combat readiness". This effect is easily verifiable - just focus your eyes and try to look away. Most likely it won't work. In addition, the described expression is unlikely to allow you to breathe more intensively, speak in a high voice, or tilt your head to your shoulder.

Remember: a slight smile automatically makes you look more welcoming.

4.4. Treacherous facial expressions

You already know that in some situations, posture and gestures can completely expose a person. The same can be said about our unconscious facial expressions when, for example, we flirt or do not want to finish everything.

Facial expressions that can reveal

Even the slightest twitch of the facial muscles or blinking of the eyes can arouse the suspicion that the speaker is faking or hiding something.
Here are the signs by which deceit or pretense is recognized:

• The interlocutor blinks his eyes unusually often.

• He has an unnatural expression on his face, something like a wide grin.

• He avoids direct eye contact, literally "doesn't dare to look you in the eye."

• He often closes his eyes.

There are 43 muscles in the face, more than anywhere else in our body. Therefore, the possibilities of facial expression in humans are almost unlimited and, moreover, if we take into account the existence of numerous cultural characteristics, they are very diverse. Despite this, knowing a few simple rules usually helps you better understand people, especially when you first meet.

• A closed facial expression - that is, tightly compressed lips and a fixed look - is an unequivocal refusal, rejection.

• A smile is only perceived as sincere when the eyes smile along with the lips (small wrinkles form around the eyes).

• Highly raised eyebrows indicate surprise and interest.

• You can influence your state of mind not only through posture and gestures, but also through facial expressions. A smile automatically improves mood, and a gloomy facial expression, on the contrary, has a depressing effect on the psyche.

5. Differences in body language due to cultural differences.

There are no patented recipes for interpreting body language. Sometimes a certain gesture or facial expression may seem unambiguous to us, but in fact, for their correct interpretation, many factors must be taken into account.

Along with age and gender, cultural affiliation of a person also belongs to such factors.

To understand how much this aspect affects body language, it is enough to mention that in bilingual people, posture, gestures and facial expressions change depending on what language they are speaking at the moment.

What misunderstandings can lead to ignorance of the features of body language that exist in other cultures, shows the following example.

An American lawyer, who accompanied the governor of one of the states during his visit to Japan, delivered a speech there to the highest officials of the state administration.

The reaction of the audience left the lawyer completely convinced that his report had bored the listeners so much that they simply fell asleep.

This man did not know that closed eyes and a slight affirmative shake of the head are in Japan the sign of the most concentrated attention.

5.1. How to say hello in different parts of the world

What do you think could happen if you put your foot on a person's head as a sign of greeting? Surely he would not be delighted with this - unlike the representatives of the South Indian Toda tribe, where such a manner of greeting younger members of the tribe is a common occurrence.

There are many diverse greeting rituals in the world, and how can one not recall the saying: "Whatever the edge, then its own custom."

• In both Europe and America, people shake hands, take off their

hats, or touch them when they meet.
• In Great Britain it is limited to a slight nod.
• The Chinese, greeting, bow low.
• In India and Southeast Asia, it is customary to put your palms together.
• Moroccans greet each other with a kiss on the hand.
• The custom of kissing the hand has survived to this day also in Central Europe and Latin America.

Differences in the forms of greeting are due to the cultural characteristics of the peoples. Going on a trip, ask how it is customary to greet in a particular country: will one handshake be enough or is it necessary to kiss the hand.

5.2. Consent and refusal

We learn individual "words" of body language in the first year of life. And above all else - nodding or shaking the head as signs of confirmation or denial. In most countries of the world, these signals are endowed with the same meaning. However, there are exceptions.

• To show agreement, in India, Pakistan and Bulgaria they shake their heads from side to side, and in Ethiopia they throw their heads back.

• And in Greece, Turkey and Southern Italy, for example, throwing the head back means denial or rejection.

• Almost as common as shaking one's head is the expression of disagreement in the world through the negative movement of the hand or index finger, as well as through the crossing of the arms.

• A special gesture is used for this purpose in southern Italy and in Sardinia - they quickly pass their hand over the chin from the bottom up.

• In Japan, the signal of denial and disagreement is the fanning of the hand.

5.3. Misunderstandings can be avoided

Numerous unconscious gestures that we constantly resort to in everyday life are also characteristic of other cultures. But, unfortunately, this does not always facilitate mutual understanding. Very often the same gesture in another cultural space is understood in a completely different way than ours. And if you proceed from the fact that a certain gesture has the same meaning everywhere, then you are at great risk and can easily get into a mess.

Here are some examples of different interpretations of gestures in different cultural contexts.

• A person typically touches their interlocutor about 180 times in an hour, while in the UK they don't touch at all. And if you imagine a conversation between an Englishman and a Puerto Rican, then the first, most likely, will experience significant discomfort from annoying touches, and the second will get the impression that he is completely unsympathetic to his interlocutor.

• Connecting the thumb and forefinger to form an "O" is considered a positive sign of approval in North America and Europe. For the Japanese, it is a symbol of money. In France, Belgium and Tunisia, such a combination of fingers is associated with zero and is perceived as a derogatory assessment. In Malta, Greece, Tunisia, Turkey, some countries in South America and the Middle East, this gesture is regarded as obscene and offensive.

• The thumbs up is a symbol of approval almost everywhere in the world. In Japan, this is the number five. And in Australia and Nigeria, they stick out their thumbs when they want an unpleasant interlocutor to disappear as soon as possible.
• In most countries, the gesture in the form of the Latin letter "V"

(the first letter of the word "Victory") with the index and middle fingers raised up is understood as "victory" or "peace." And only in the UK and Australia is this an impolite way to make it clear to the interlocutor that they do not want to do business with him anymore.

When in a foreign country or communicating with foreign business partners, do not use gestures whose local meaning you do not know exactly. In such cases, it is recommended to gesticulate as discreetly as possible - this reduces the risk of being misunderstood.

6. Test: are you good at body language

Well, now it's up to you! You just spent 30 minutes learning something new about posture, gestures and facial expressions.

The short quiz below will help you determine how "fluent" your body language is.

A few preliminary remarks

When exercising, there are five important factors to consider:

1. In most cases, the context is rather sharp, tense situations (for example, commercial negotiations, an interview in the personnel department, etc.).

2.Any physical defects are not taken into account in principle.

3.As a rule, we are talking about unconscious body signals.

4.One should proceed from those semantic meanings of postures, gestures and facial expressions that are accepted in our cultural space.
    5.All the described body signals are not individual habits of

the interlocutors.